MULA MOMMA

The Household Systems Method™

BY

REHANA SEWOATSRI

TABLE OF CONTENTS

INTRODUCTION

We were sitting at dinner.
Phones were supposed to be away.
One of the kids refused.

I felt it immediately.
That tightness.
Irritation.
A flash of something that felt bigger than the moment itself.

And underneath that,
hesitation.

Because part of me didn't want to push it.
Didn't want to create tension.
Didn't want to overstep.
Didn't want to be "too much."

And part of me knew exactly what was happening.

So I said it.

"If you want that drink tonight,
it's coming out of your money."

The table went quiet.
Dinner finished.

We got in the car.
No one said much.

And somewhere between the restaurant and home,
I heard it.

Not out loud.
But clear enough that I couldn't ignore it.

My mother's voice.

The way money used to show up when I was growing up.
The way it carried weight.
Pressure.
Sometimes control.

And in that moment, I realized something that changed how I saw everything.
Not just that interaction.
Not just that night.
Everything.

If I wasn't intentional,
those patterns would move through me into them.

Not because I wanted them to.
Because that's what patterns do.

They don't stop on their own.
They move.
From one generation to the next.
Unless someone interrupts them.

That was the moment I stopped looking at our household as a collection of personalities trying to get along.

And started seeing it for what it actually was.

A system.

A system with:
expectations
incentives
gaps
and inconsistencies

And once I saw it that way,
I couldn't unsee it.

Because the truth is,
most of the tension inside modern households isn't emotional.
It's structural.

We think it's attitude.
We think it's personality.
We think it's disrespect.
We think it's the complexity of blending families.

But what I've seen, over and over again, is something much simpler.

When structure is missing:
Expectations become unclear.
Responsibility becomes inconsistent.
Decisions become emotional.
People stop leading.
And start reacting.

That's where tension lives.
Not in the people.
In the absence of structure.

The problem isn't that women don't care.
The problem isn't that families are too complex.
The problem is that no one ever taught us how to lead here.

In our careers, we're given playbooks.
We learn how to:
run meetings
set expectations
design systems
manage people

But inside our homes?
Especially in blended families,
we're handed complexity...
and expected to improvise.

Two households.
Different expectations.
Different rules.
Different financial habits.
Different authority dynamics.

And the same children moving between all of it.
Trying to figure out:
What matters.
What's consistent.
What the rules actually are.

So we try to hold it together.
We soften.
We avoid friction.
We question ourselves.
We wonder if we're doing too much.
Or not enough.

And slowly,
without realizing it,
we allow ambiguity to lead.

This book exists to change that.

Not by telling you to parent harder.
Not by giving you scripts or quick fixes.
But by showing you something more powerful.

How to see your household clearly.
How to understand what's actually happening beneath the surface.
And how to build the kind of structure that makes leadership possible.

Because this isn't just about getting through the day.
It's about what your home is producing.

The behaviors.
The expectations.
The patterns.
The adults your children will eventually become.

And that doesn't happen by accident.
It happens by design.

This isn't parenting.

This is systems.

CHAPTER 1

This Wasn't About Behavior

We were in the kitchen.
Backpacks on the floor.
Shoes still on.
Dinner hadn't even started.

And the tension was already there.

It was small.
A tone.
A response.
A look that stayed too long.

I felt it immediately.
That tightness.
Irritation.
And underneath it,
hesitation.

Because part of me didn't want to say anything.
Didn't want to create friction.
Didn't want to make something small... bigger.

And part of me knew,
this wasn't small.

I stood there, watching it play out.

Waiting.
Hoping it would correct itself.

It didn't.

So I said it.

"Go put your shoes away.
Then come back."

It wasn't the instruction.
It was the reaction.

That pause.
That resistance.
The shift that said,
this isn't about the shoes.

And I felt it again.
Stronger.
Not irritation.
Recognition.

Because I had seen this before.
Not here.
In rooms where things looked fine,
and nothing was actually working.

Unclear expectations.
Shifting roles.
Decisions based on mood.

Same result.
Every time.

Confusion.
Inconsistency.

Tension that kept repeating.

And that's when it clicked.

This wasn't behavior.
This was structure.
Or more accurately,
the absence of it.

Because behavior doesn't exist on its own.
It responds.
To what's clear.
To what's consistent.
To what's reinforced.

And when those aren't stable,
behavior won't be either.

But we misread it.

Disrespect.
Defiance.
Attitude.

We make it personal.

When what we're actually seeing,
is a system producing exactly what it was built to produce.
Even if no one built it intentionally.

That's the shift.

Because once you see your household as a system,
you stop taking everything personally.
You stop reacting to every moment like it's isolated.
And you start asking a different question.

Not:
"What's wrong with them?"

But:
"What is this environment producing?"

Because every household is producing something.
Clarity or confusion.
Consistency or tension.
Responsibility or resistance.

Not randomly.
By design.

This wasn't disrespect.
It was unclear expectations.

And once I saw that,
I couldn't unsee it.

CHAPTER 2

The Problem Isn't Love

We were in the car.
Quiet.
Too quiet.

Everyone was there.
No one disconnected.

And still,
something wasn't working.

That's what confused me.

Because we cared.
We showed up.
We tried.

There was no lack of love.
And the tension was still there.

In tone.
In reactions.
In moments that felt bigger than they should.

And I remember thinking,
why does this feel harder than it should?

The easy answer was already there.

Blended family.
Different backgrounds.
Different rules.
Of course it's hard.

That's what people say.
But it never fully landed.

Because I had seen complexity work.
Different people.
Different priorities.
Different pressures.

And when structure was clear,
it held.

Not perfectly.
But consistently.

And without it,
everything became harder than it should.

That's when it shifted.

This didn't feel like a love problem.
Because love was already here.

It just wasn't translating.

We were all bringing something into this space,
but there was no system translating it into something consistent.
No shared structure.
No stable expectations.
Just effort.

And effort, on its own,
isn't enough.

Because effort changes.
Energy changes.
Mood changes.
Patience changes.

And when everything depends on how someone feels in the moment,
nothing stabilizes.

That's the gap.

Love creates intention.
Structure creates consistency.

And without consistency,
nothing stabilizes.

People don't know what to expect.

And when they don't know what to expect,
they test.
Push.
Pull.
Adjust.

Not because they don't care.
Because they don't know.

That's where tension comes from.
Not lack of love.
Lack of clarity.

And once I saw that,
I started noticing it everywhere.

Moments where something small turned into something bigger,
not because it mattered that much,
but because nothing underneath it was stable.

Moments where we were all trying,
but arriving at different outcomes.
That's when the question changed.

From:
"Why is this happening?"

To:
"What is missing here?"

And the answer was always the same.

Structure.

Not more conversations.
Not more patience.
Not more understanding.

Structure.

Because structure is what takes:
intention
effort
care

...and turns it into something people can actually rely on.

Without it,
everything stays dependent on the moment.

And moments are inconsistent.

This wasn't a love issue.
It was a design issue.

And that changes everything.

Because you can't fix a structural problem with more emotion.
You can't stabilize a system with more effort.

You can't create consistency without something consistent.

This isn't about how much you care.

It's about what your environment produces.

And environments don't respond to love alone.
They respond to structure.

This isn't a love problem.

It's a structure problem.

CHAPTER 3

Why It Feels Personal (But Isn't)

It was a small moment.
A tone.
A response.
And then,
that look.

Subtle.
But enough.

I felt it immediately.

Why are they talking to me like that?

It felt sharp.
Dismissive.
And just like that,
my mind filled it in.

Disrespect.
That's what it felt like.

And underneath it,
a quieter thought.

Why does this keep happening?

That's the shift.
From moment,
to meaning.

Because once it feels personal,
everything changes.

Your tone.
Your response.
Your energy.

You stop responding to the moment.
And start responding to what you think it means.

I've seen this before.

Rooms where leaders started taking things personally.
Where feedback felt like attack.
Where behavior felt targeted.
And once that shift happened,
clarity disappeared.

Everything became about the person.
Instead of the system.

And that's what I felt happening.
In real time.

From observing,
to reacting.

And something didn't sit right.

Because if it was personal,
it would be consistent.
Same pattern.
Same intensity.

But it wasn't.

It showed up in moments.
Inconsistently.

And inconsistency doesn't come from intention.
It comes from environment.

That's the shift.

This didn't feel like disrespect.
It felt like a response.
To something unclear.

Because behavior adjusts.
To what's expected.
To what's allowed.
To what changes.

And when those change,
behavior does too.

But we take it personally.

Disrespect.
Defiance.
Attitude.

We mislabel the system.

And once we do,
we can't see it clearly.

That's the trap.
This isn't personal.
It's structural.

And once I separated myself from it,

I could actually see it.

Not as something happening to me,
but something happening within the system I was part of.

That's when the question changed.

From:
"Why are they acting like this toward me?"

To:
"What is this environment teaching?"

Because every interaction teaches something.

What matters.
What's flexible.
What's enforced.
What's optional.

Not through what we say.
Through what we consistently do.

And when that's unclear,
people fill in the gaps.

They test.
They adjust.
They respond.

Not to you,
to the system.

And that changed how I responded.

Less reaction.
More clarity.
Less emotion.

More design.

Because you can't fix something you're taking personally.
But you can redesign something once you see it clearly.

This isn't personal.
It's structural.

CHAPTER 4

The Cost Of Keeping The Peace

It was small.
A comment.
A tone.
Something that could go either way.

I heard it.
Paused.
And made a decision.

Let it go.

Not tonight.
Not over this.
Not when things feel calm.

So I moved on.
Changed the subject.
Kept it light.

And on the surface,
it worked.

No tension.
No escalation.
Everything stayed smooth.

That's what makes it convincing.

Because in the moment,
it feels like the right decision.
Like maturity.
Like restraint.
Like peace.

But later,
I felt it.
Not loud.
But there.

Because nothing resolved.
It was just avoided.

And I replayed it.
Not the comment.
The decision.

Why didn't I say anything?
The answer came fast.

Because I didn't want what came next.
The pushback.
The shift.
The discomfort.

So I chose the easier path.
Short-term peace.

And that's when it clicked.

That moment didn't disappear.
It compounded.

Because what you allow once,
becomes possible.

What you allow twice,
becomes a pattern.

What you never address,
becomes the standard.

Not because anyone said it out loud.
Because the system absorbed it.

That's the cost.
Not the moment you avoid.
What that avoidance builds.

Because every time you let something slide,
the system adjusts.

Expectations shift.
Boundaries soften.
Clarity fades.
Quietly.

And the next time it happens,
it's harder to address.
Because now it's not new.
It's familiar.

That's how inconsistency builds.
Not in big moments.
In small ones.
Repeated.

Until one day,
you're not responding to a moment.
You're reacting to a pattern.

That's when it feels heavy.

Not because it is,
because it's been reinforced.

Avoiding conflict doesn't remove tension.
It relocates it.

From the moment,
into the system.

And once it's there,
it shows up everywhere.

Different situations.
Same pattern.

That's the signal.

Because a system can't hold a standard,
that isn't consistently enforced.

And the real cost isn't what you avoided.
It's what you quietly shaped.

Not in how I handled big moments.
In how I handled small ones.
The ones that feel easy to ignore.
The ones that don't seem worth addressing.
The ones that quietly shape everything over time.

Because those are the moments that define the system.
Not the loud ones.
The consistent ones.

This isn't peace.

It's delayed conflict.

And delayed conflict always collects interest.

Real peace doesn't come from avoiding tension.
It comes from removing ambiguity.

And ambiguity only disappears,
when structure replaces it.

CHAPTER 5

Kids Don't Resist Structure

We were at the table.
Homework open.
Pencils out.

"Finish this first.
Then you can go."

Simple.
Clear.

It should've taken ten minutes.
It didn't.

A sigh.
A delay.
"Do I have to do it right now?"

And there it was.
That shift.

Not loud.
Just enough resistance to change the moment.

I felt it immediately.

Here we go.

Because this is where it usually goes next.

Push.
Pause.
Repeat.

And before you know it,
you're negotiating something that was never supposed to be a negotiation.

That's what it looks like.
Resistance.
They don't want to listen.
They don't like structure.

That's what it feels like.

And for a long time,
that's what I believed.

That structure creates pushback.

So I adjusted.
Softened the ask.
Delayed the timing.
Added flexibility.
Trying to reduce friction.

And for a moment,
it worked.

Until it didn't.

Because the resistance didn't disappear.
It moved.
Later.
Different moment.
Same pattern.

That's what made me stop.

Because if structure was the problem,
removing it should've fixed it.

It didn't.
It made it worse.

That's when I started paying attention.
Not just to behavior,
to when it showed up.
And when it didn't.

Moments where things were clear,
and stayed clear,
looked different.

Less negotiation.
Less pushback.

Not perfect.
But stable.

And moments where things shifted,
based on mood, timing, energy,
looked the same.

More questions.
More testing.

That's where the resistance lived.
Not in the structure.
In the inconsistency of it.

That's the shift.

This isn't resistance to structure.

It's a response to ambiguity.

Because when expectations aren't stable,
people don't know where the edge is.

So they look for it.

They test.
Not to challenge authority.
To understand it.

Where does this apply?
When does this matter?

And every time the answer changes,
the testing continues.

Not because something is wrong.
Because something is unclear.

That's what I hadn't seen.

I thought the pushback meant I needed to soften.
It didn't.
It meant I needed to stabilize.

Because real structure doesn't create tension.
It removes it.

It answers the question before it's asked.
It eliminates the need to test.
Because the edge is already visible.

And once that edge is clear,
behavior stabilizes.
Not immediately.
Not perfectly.
But predictably.

Because people adjust to what they can rely on.
Not what changes.

That's the shift.

I stopped trying to reduce resistance,
and started trying to increase clarity.

Stopped softening expectations,
and started stabilizing them.

Because the goal isn't to eliminate pushback.
It's about creating an environment they don't have to question.

This isn't resistance.

It's ambiguity.

And ambiguity,
always gets tested.

Kids don't resist structure.
They resist not knowing where it actually is.

. . .

CHAPTER 6

Money Is Never Just Money

We were in the store.

"Can I get this?"

Small.
A snack.
A drink.

It shouldn't have mattered.

But I paused.

Not because of the item.
Because of everything underneath it.

Because that question isn't just a question.
It's a signal.

I had seen this before.
Not in stores.
In rooms where money decisions weren't about money.

Where a yes or no,
meant something else.

Access.
Control.
Expectation.

And standing there,
I realized,
this wasn't about the snack.
It was about the system.

Because in a system without structure,
every decision becomes situational.

One day yes.
One day no.
Same question.
Different outcome.

That's not flexibility.
That's unpredictability.

And unpredictability creates something fast.
Confusion.

Because when something changes,
people don't adjust to it.
They test it.

Where is the line?
What actually applies?

And when the answer keeps shifting,
behavior keeps adjusting.

That's the tension.
Not the request.
The lack of clarity around it.

I had seen this play out in bigger ways.
Subscriptions no one realized were active.
Duplicate purchases across households.

Money being spent,
without anyone fully owning the decision.

Not because people didn't care.
Because there was no system holding it.

No visibility.
No structure connecting:
what's available
what's allowed
what's expected

So everything stayed reactive.
Moment by moment.
Decision by decision.

That's when I saw it clearly.

Money isn't just money.
It's a mirror.

It shows:
What's clear.
What's assumed.
What's inconsistent.
And most importantly, what's unclear.

And most households don't have a money problem.
They have a visibility problem.

Because when money isn't structured,
it doesn't feel real.
It feels flexible.
Available.
Until it's not.

And that shift,
feels abrupt.
Not because the rule changed.
Because the structure never existed.

That's when I stopped answering the question,
and started answering the system.

"How are you planning to pay for it?"

Pause.
Shift.

Because now,
it's not about getting.
It's about understanding.

Because structure determines:
whether money creates tension, or clarity.
Whether it reinforces entitlement, or responsibility.
Whether it feels unpredictable, or stable.

And most households,
aren't struggling with money itself.
They're struggling with what money is revealing.

That's what shows up in those small moments.
The ones that seem insignificant.
The ones that feel like quick decisions.

Because they're not just decisions.
They're signals.

Repeated.
Reinforced.
Observed.

And over time,
they become the system.

This isn't spending.

It's behavior.

And behavior,
always follows structure.

. . .

CHAPTER 7

The Invisible System Running Your Home

It was a Saturday.
No schedule.
No pressure.
Just a normal day.

Which is where things start to slip.

Questions.

"Can I do this?"
"Do I have to do that?"

Small.
Constant.

And I answered them.

Yes.
No.
Maybe later.

Adjusting in real time.

And for a while,
it worked.

Until it didn't.

Because at some point,
the answers started colliding.

"You said I could, "
"That's not what you told me, "

And suddenly,
I wasn't answering questions.
I was managing confusion.

That's the moment that stopped me.

Because nothing had gone wrong.
No argument.
No big decision.

And still,
everything felt off.

That's when it clicked.

This wasn't random.
This was a system.
Just not an intentional one.

Because every household has a system.
Designed,
or defaulted.

And default systems follow one rule.
Whatever is easiest in the moment.

That's what I was doing.
Managing moments.
Instead of building structure.

And the system responded.

Because when decisions are made moment-to-moment,
nothing holds.

And when nothing holds,
people stop relying.
They start checking.
Constantly.

Is this still true?
Does this apply right now?

That's not defiance.
That's calibration.

They're trying to understand the system.
Because nothing is stable enough to rely on.

I had seen this before.
In businesses where nothing was documented.
Where every decision lived in someone's head.
Where people had to ask before they acted,
because nothing existed outside of the moment.

And those systems always felt the same.
Heavy.
Reactive.
Dependent.

Not because people weren't capable.
Because nothing was clear.

That's why it feels exhausting.

Because you're not answering questions.
You're acting as the system.
Holding everything.

In real time.

And the moment you stop,
everything collapses.

That's not a system.
That's dependency.

And dependency doesn't scale.
It drains.

Here's what most people miss.

Clarity in the moment,
is not the same as clarity in the system.

And that's where most people get stuck.
We think if we say it once, it's understood.
If we handle it once, it's solved.

But systems don't respond to one-time decisions.
They respond to repeated structure.

What's visible.
What's consistent.
What doesn't change depending on the day.

That's what creates stability.
Not effort.
Not intention.
Structure.

This isn't chaos.

It's an unmanaged system.
And unmanaged systems,
always produce visible problems.

CHAPTER 8

You're Not "Too Much"

It was a small moment.
A correction.
A boundary.
Nothing dramatic.

And then,
that shift.

A look.
A pause.
Subtle.
But enough.

Enough to feel it.

And immediately,
I felt it too.

Was that too much?

It happens fast.

You say something.
Clear.
Direct.

And within seconds,

you're not thinking about the decision.
You're thinking about how it landed.
How it felt.
How it was received.

And then,
you adjust.

Maybe I should've said it differently.
Maybe I should've waited.

Because the last thing you want,
is to create tension.

Especially in a blended household.
Where everything already feels like it requires balance.
Awareness.
Care.
Restraint.

So you soften.
Not all at once.
Just enough.

Tone.
Timing.
Delivery.

And from the outside,
it looks like awareness.
Patience.
Flexibility.

But internally,
it feels different.

It feels like holding back.
Like you're editing yourself in real time.

Am I being too strict?
Too structured?
Too direct?
Am I doing too much?

That question sits underneath everything.
Quiet.
But constant.

That's where hesitation starts.
Not in what's right.
In whether you should act on it.

Because once hesitation enters,
clarity weakens.

And when clarity weakens,
the system shifts.

Boundaries stretch.
Expectations move.
Not loudly.
Quietly.

Until what was clear,
becomes negotiable.

That's when things feel off.
Not chaotic.
Inconsistent.

And now you're repeating yourself.
Re-explaining.

Re-deciding.
Wondering why nothing sticks.

This is where most people misread it.

They think:
"I'm doing too much."

That's not the problem.

The problem is,
nothing is holding what you set.

Because when structure is strong,
you don't carry every moment.
The system does.

It reinforces.
It stabilizes.
It holds.

But when structure is weak,
you become the system.

And everything depends on you.
Your tone.
Your energy.
Your timing.

That's what feels heavy.
Not leadership.
Lack of support.

That's not a place where you shrink.
That's not a place where you soften.

Because it's not anchored to anything.

It's just you.
In the moment.
Holding it.

The question isn't:
"How do I soften this?"

The question is:
"How do I stabilize this?"

Because leadership doesn't require you to shrink.
It requires the system to expand.
To support it.
To reinforce it.
To make it sustainable.

You're not too much.
You're just unsupported.

And unsupported leadership,
always feels like pressure.

Because nothing is holding it.

This isn't about softening yourself.

It's about strengthening the system.

Because when the system holds,
you don't have to.

. . .

CHAPTER 9

You Always Had A Role

We were in the car.
A conversation started in the back.
Small.
Easy to ignore.

And I did.

I stayed quiet.
Hands on the wheel.
Eyes forward.
Let it play out.

Because it wasn't directed at me.
Not my place.

That's what I told myself.

And for a moment,
it felt easier.

No tension.
No interruption.
Just let it pass.

But it didn't pass.
It built.

Tone shifted.
Energy changed.

And I felt it.

Something isn't right.

And still,
I hesitated.

Because this is the line.
The one that feels hardest to navigate.

Where do I step in?
Where do I stay back?

Especially here.
Where roles feel... unclear.
Where authority can feel conditional.
Where you're constantly aware of not overstepping.

So you adjust.
You observe.
You wait.

Telling yourself:
"It's not my place."

But that's the illusion.

Because whether you act,
or don't,
you're still part of the system.

And systems don't recognize intention.
They respond to participation.

That's the shift.

There is no neutral position.

You're either reinforcing something,
or allowing it.

Either way,
you're shaping it.

That's what I hadn't fully owned.
I thought silence removed me.
It didn't.
It contributed.

Because what's not addressed,
becomes acceptable.

What's not clarified,
becomes flexible.

What's not led,
leads itself.

That's the system.
Not intentional.
But consistent.

And somewhere in that car,
I had been borrowing clarity.
Letting someone else define the expectations.
Letting the moment decide what I was allowed to do.

And calling it respect.

That's when the question changed.

Not:
"Is this my place?"

But:
"What is my role here?"

Because the role already exists.

You don't choose whether you influence the system.
You choose whether it's intentional.

And kids are not waiting for you to figure it out.
They're reading the room.
They're assigning meaning to your presence.

And if you haven't decided what your role is,
they will.

And what they create won't feel like structure.
It will feel like uncertainty.

Because what they're responding to,
is a system without ownership.

And a system without ownership,
doesn't feel flexible.

It feels unsafe.

That's leadership.

Not stepping into everything.
But being clear where it matters.
Consistent enough,
that the system recognizes it.

Because once you claim your role,
the system starts to organize around it.

Not perfectly.
Not immediately.

But noticeably.

Less hesitation.
More clarity.

Because now,
you're not reacting to the system.
You're shaping it.

This isn't about stepping in more.

It's about realizing,
you were never out of it.

You always had a role.
The only question was,
whether you were using it on purpose.

. . .

CHAPTER 10

Borrowed Clarity

There was a rule already in place.
I didn't set it.
I didn't question it.
I just... worked around it.

Something small had come up,
a decision that needed to be made.
And I knew what I thought.
I knew what made sense to me.

But I paused.
Not because I was unsure.
Because I wasn't sure it was mine to say.

So I waited.
I watched.
I adjusted myself to fit what was already there.

. . .

I told myself it was respect.
That I was being thoughtful.
That it wasn't my place to rewrite rules I hadn't written.

And I believed that.
For longer than I want to admit.

Because from the outside,
it looked like patience.
It looked like grace.
It looked like the kind of awareness that blended families require.

But underneath,
something else was happening.

I kept deferring.
Not in moments.
As a posture.

Waiting to see what the rules were.
Adjusting to what already existed.
Trying to find where I fit,
instead of deciding where I stood.

And the quiet question underneath all of it,
the one I didn't say out loud:

Is this mine to hold?

. . .

So I let it go.
Not loudly.
Not dramatically.
I just didn't claim it.

I followed the tone that was already there.
I matched the energy of the room.
I operated inside a definition I never wrote.

And I called it fitting in.

. . .

I had seen this before.
Not here.
In organizations where decisions lived in someone else's head.
Where people adjusted to the room instead of directing it.
Where no one had claimed ownership of the system,
so everyone borrowed from whoever seemed most certain.

And those systems always felt the same.
Unclear.
Reactive.
Unstable in ways that were hard to name
but impossible to ignore.

And standing there,
I felt it.
That quiet click.
Not loud.
Almost uncomfortable.

I hadn't been absent from the system.
I had been operating inside someone else's version of it.

Taking my cues from what was already there.
Waiting to see what was allowed.
Letting someone else's clarity become mine.

That's not deference.
That's borrowed clarity.

And borrowed clarity,
I realized,
can be revised.
Revoked.
Reinterpreted.
Without notice.

Because it was never mine to begin with.

. . .

You cannot build a system
on something you don't own.

Borrowed clarity feels like fitting in.
But what it actually does
is remove you from the equation.

Because when someone else defines the expectations,
you don't hold them.
You inherit them.

And inherited systems
don't respond to you.
They respond to whoever wrote them.

That's where instability comes from.
Not from the people.
Not from the complexity.
From operating inside a system
that no one in the room actually owns.

When clarity is borrowed,
it shifts with whoever holds it.

And when it shifts,
everything underneath it shifts too.

Expectations move.
Standards soften.
Behavior adjusts to the instability.

And the tension that follows,

feels personal.
But it's structural.

This is what most households don't see.
They think the problem is love.
Or effort.
Or personality.

But most households don't struggle because people don't care.
They struggle because clarity is borrowed
instead of owned.

And borrowed clarity,
is why the system never holds.

. . .

This isn't patience.

It's operating without ownership.

This isn't respect.

It's deferring permanently.

This isn't fitting in.

It's borrowed clarity.

And once you see that,
the question changes.

Not:
Where do I fit?

But:
What do I own?

Owned clarity doesn't have to be loud.

It doesn't have to be forceful.
It doesn't have to rewrite everything that came before it.

It just has to be yours.
Decided.
Defined.
Held.

Because a system built on owned clarity
doesn't shift when someone else's changes.

It holds.
Not because you forced it.
Because you built it.

And what's built,
is what they grow inside of.
What they absorb without knowing it.
What they carry forward,
long after you're not the one explaining it.

That's the weight of this.
Not pressure.
Clarity.

Because borrowed clarity doesn't just fail you.
It fails them.

CHAPTER 11

Structure Is Not Control

It was late.
The house was quiet.
The kind of quiet that comes after a full day.

And one moment stayed with me.

A boundary.
Simple.
Clear.
I held it.
Calm.
Direct.

And then,
the shift.

A look.
A pause.
Subtle resistance.

And I felt it.

Was that too much?

That thought didn't come from nowhere.
It came from years of awareness.

Of reading the room.
Of adjusting tone.
Of softening edges before they even formed.

Because somewhere along the way,
we learn something.

That structure feels like control.
That holding a boundary feels like force.
That clarity might create distance.

And in a blended household,
that awareness gets sharper.
Because nothing feels neutral.
Everything feels like it carries weight.

So you adjust.
Soften it.
Delay it.
Reconsider what you were already clear on.

Because you don't want to disrupt the moment.

And in doing that,
you create something else.

Instability.

Because what's not held,
doesn't stay clear.
It shifts.

And once it shifts,
it becomes negotiable.

That's the problem.
Not the boundary.

The movement of it.

Because when something moves,
people test it.
Push it.
Revisit it.
Trying to understand where it actually is.

That's where tension comes from.
Not structure.
Ambiguity.

That's the shift.

Because control and structure are not the same thing.

Control tries to force behavior.
Structure makes behavior predictable.

Control depends on constant enforcement.
Structure creates consistency without constant effort.

Control is reactive.
Structure is designed.

And I had been treating them like they were the same.
That's why it felt heavy.
That's why it felt like every moment required energy.

Because without structure,
everything has to be managed in real time.
Every boundary.
Every expectation.
Every decision.

Held.
Explained.

Reinforced.
Again and again.

And when that happens,
of course it feels like control.
Because there's nothing else holding it.

When structure is missing,
you become the structure.

And when you become the structure,
everything depends on you.
Your tone.
Your timing.
Your energy.

And that's exhausting.
Not because leadership is heavy,
but because it's unsupported.

That's when I saw it clearly.
This wasn't about being too firm.
It wasn't about being too structured.
It wasn't about creating tension.
It was about removing ambiguity.

Because ambiguity creates instability.
And instability creates tension.

Structure removes it.
Not with force.
With clarity.

Because real structure doesn't feel forceful.
It feels clear.
It doesn't need to be re-explained every time.

It doesn't shift depending on the moment.
It holds.

Quietly.
Consistently.

And when something holds,
people adjust to it.
Not because they're being controlled.
Because they understand it.
Because they can rely on it.
Because it doesn't change.

That's the shift.

This isn't control.

It's care.

Because structure isn't control.
It's what allows everything else to function without it.

It's what turns intention into consistency.
Clarity into stability.
Leadership into something that doesn't have to be carried,
moment by moment.

And once I understood that,
I stopped pulling back from it.
And started building it.

. . .

CHAPTER 12

Consistency Is The Real Authority

It was late.
Everyone was tired.
That kind of tired where everything feels slightly heavier than it should.

And it started with something small.

A reminder.
Something that had already been said.

"Hey, remember what we talked about?"

Calm.
Clear.
Nothing extra.

A pause.
A response that sounded like agreement.

And then,
nothing.

No movement.
No follow-through.

I felt it immediately.

That shift.

I already said this.
Why am I saying it again?

That's the moment.
The one most people miss.

Not the first time.
The second.

Because the first time feels like leadership.
The second time starts to feel like something else.

Like you're not being heard.
Like it didn't land.
Like it doesn't carry weight.

And that's when tone changes.
Slightly.
More direct.
More force.

Because now you're not stating.
You're trying to make it stick.

And the more you try to make it stick in the moment, the heavier it feels.

This is where most people misread it.

They think:
"They're not listening."

But that's not the problem.

The problem isn't listening.
The problem is consistency.

Because clarity once,
is not clarity in a system.

Clarity once is a moment.
Consistency creates structure.

And without structure,
everything resets.
Every time.

Same expectation.
New moment.
No carryover.

So nothing builds.
Nothing holds.
Nothing stabilizes.

That's why it keeps repeating.
Not because it wasn't heard.
Because it wasn't anchored.

This is where authority actually comes from.
Not tone.
Not volume.
Not repetition.

Consistency.

Consistency removes the question.
And when the question is gone,
behavior adjusts.

Not immediately.
But predictably.

That's the shift.

I stopped trying to make moments land harder,
and started making them land the same.

Same expectation.
Same response.
Same outcome.

Not perfectly.
But predictably.

And that's when things started to stabilize.
Less repetition.
Less tension.
Less need to escalate something that should have been simple.

Because now the system was holding it.
Not me.

When the system holds it,
you don't have to.
You don't have to increase your tone.
You don't have to add more explanation.
You don't have to carry the weight of every moment.

It's already built in.
Already understood.
Already reinforced.

Consistent.
Quiet.
Unmoving.

Clear enough that it doesn't have to be questioned.

Because once something is consistent,
it becomes predictable.

And once it's predictable,
it becomes reliable.

And once it's reliable,
it becomes respected.

Not because it's demanded.
Because it's experienced.

That's the shift.

You're not trying to get them to listen better.
You're giving them something stable enough,
that they don't have to question it.

That's what authority is.
Not what you say.
What stays the same.

And what stays the same,
is what gets respected.

. . .

CHAPTER 13

Visibility Changes Behavior

"Do I still have money left?"

Simple question.

I paused.
Not because I didn't want to answer.
Because I didn't know.

Not clearly.
Not in a way that could be seen.

And that's when it hit me.

If the answer depends on memory,
it's not a system.
It's a guess.

And guesses don't create stability.
They create hesitation.

I answered anyway.
Estimated.
Filled the gap.
Moved on.

But the moment didn't move on.

Because I had seen this before.

Not in homes.
In rooms where numbers weren't visible.
Everything felt fine,
until it wasn't.
Because nothing was actually being seen.

We weren't lacking discipline.
We were lacking visibility.

Because behavior doesn't stabilize around what's hidden.
It stabilizes around what's seen.

What's visible, gets adjusted.
What's invisible, gets ignored.

Not intentionally.
Consistently.

That's what was happening.
Questions instead of clarity.
Checking instead of knowing.

And every time that happens,
the system resets.
Because nothing is holding.

So I changed one thing.
Not more explanation.
Not more reminders.

Visibility.

"What's available is here."

Not in my head.
Not in a conversation.
In front of us.

And everything shifted.

Fewer questions.
Less negotiation.

Because now,
the answer didn't depend on me.

That's the shift.

Visibility removes dependency.

Because when something can be seen,
it doesn't have to be managed.

It holds.

And what holds,
changes behavior.

I expanded it beyond money.
Into everything.

Expectations.
Responsibilities.
Access.
What's allowed.
What's earned.
What's consistent.

All of it.
Made visible.
Not complicated.
Just clear enough that it didn't have to be questioned.

And the shift was immediate.
Not perfect.

But stable.

Because now,
the system wasn't invisible anymore.
It was present.

And when a system is present,
it starts doing the work for you.

Holding expectations.
Reinforcing boundaries.
Reducing friction before it starts.

Less explaining.
Less correcting.
Less reacting.

More clarity.
More consistency.
More ease.

This isn't communication.

It's visibility.

And visibility,
is what makes a system hold.

. . .

CHAPTER 14

Privileges Must Be Designed

"Can I go?"

Simple question.

I almost said yes.
Quick.
Automatic.

Because that's what these moments usually are.
Fast decisions.
Based on the moment.

But something made me pause.

Not the question.
The assumption.

Because it didn't feel like a request.
It felt like access.
Like something already available,
just waiting for confirmation.

That's when it clicked.

This wasn't about where they were going.
It was about what they believed they had access to.

This is where most people miss it.

They think the issue is behavior.
It's not.

The issue is design.

Because when access isn't defined,
it becomes assumed.

And what's assumed,
becomes expected.

Not loudly.
Quietly.

That's how entitlement forms.
Not from giving too much.
From giving without structure.

Every "can I" becomes a signal.
Every "yes" becomes a reinforcement.
Every "no" becomes a disruption,
if there was no structure before it.

That's the friction.
Not the decision itself,
the shift in expectation.

So I didn't answer the question.
I answered the system.

"What needs to be done before that happens?"

Pause.
Not resistance.
Recalibration.

Because now the moment changed.

Not permission.
Process.

And process changes everything.

Because what's designed,
becomes predictable.

And what's predictable,
people organize around.

That's what removes tension.
Not saying yes.
Not saying no.
Clarity.

Because clarity removes assumption.
And assumption is what creates misalignment.

This isn't about access.

It's about architecture.

And once the architecture is in place,
the decisions almost make themselves.

Because into how they make decisions.
Into how they handle access.
Into how they understand what's earned,
and what's expected.

Because what you build here,
doesn't stay here.

It moves with them.
Into every environment they enter.
Every system they're part of.

Every decision they make when you're not there.

That's what this becomes.
Bigger than the house.
Bigger than the moment.
Bigger than the question.

This isn't about saying yes or no.

It's about building a system that answers before the question is asked.

Because when privileges are designed,
behavior doesn't have to be managed.

It aligns.

And alignment,
is what creates ease.

This isn't about access.

It's about architecture.

. . .

CHAPTER 15

Behavior Follows Reinforcement

It didn't happen once.
It happened again.

Same behavior.
Different day.

That's what made me pause.

Because the first time,
you explain it.
They didn't know.
They forgot.
It was a one-off.

The second time,
it's a pattern.

And patterns don't repeat by accident.
They repeat by reinforcement.

I went back to the first moment.
What I said.
What I didn't say.
What I addressed.
What I let go.

Because behavior doesn't just show up.

It follows something.

Not intention.
Not conversation.
Reinforcement.

This is where most people miss it.

They think behavior follows rules.
It doesn't.

It follows what consistently happens after the rule.

What's addressed.
What's delayed.
What's ignored.

That's the system.
And reinforcement isn't always obvious.
It's not just rewards.
It's not just consequences.

It's subtler than that.

Silence.
Delay.
Inconsistency.

That's reinforcement.

If something happens,
and nothing follows,
that's reinforcement.

If something happens,
and the response changes,
that's reinforcement.

If something happens,
and it depends on the moment,
that's reinforcement.

Because from the system's perspective,
anything not clearly interrupted...
is allowed.

And anything allowed,
is repeatable.

That's what I saw.
Not the behavior.
The pathway.

I thought I was reinforcing expectations.
I wasn't.
I was reinforcing flexibility.

Sometimes I held it.
Sometimes I didn't.
Sometimes I addressed it immediately.
Sometimes I waited.

Same expectation.
Different outcomes.

And the system adjusted.
Not to the rule.
To the inconsistency of it.

That's what behavior follows.
Not what you say.
What consistently happens after.

And here's what makes it uncomfortable.

Because from your perspective,
you're clear.
You've said it.
You've addressed it.
You've explained it.

But from the system's perspective,
it's inconsistent.

And inconsistency creates instability.
And instability creates testing.

Not because someone is trying to challenge you.
Because they're trying to understand what actually holds.

So I stopped asking:
"Why does this keep happening?"

And started asking:
"What is this being reinforced by?"

Because if the reinforcement stays the same,
the behavior will too.

And most households,
aren't designed around reinforcement.
They're designed around reaction.

Moment by moment.
Which means reinforcement is happening,
by default.
Not by design.

And default systems don't produce intentional outcomes.
They produce whatever is easiest to maintain.

You don't change behavior first.

You change what reinforces it.

Because once reinforcement changes,
behavior has to adjust.
It doesn't have another option.

That's how systems work.

What's reinforced becomes expected.
What's expected becomes automatic.
What's automatic,
doesn't need to be managed.

That's the goal.

This isn't about correcting behavior.

It's about controlling what gets repeated.

And what gets repeated,
is always tied to reinforcement.

This isn't behavior.

It's reinforcement.

And reinforcement,
is what your household is built on.

. . .

CHAPTER 16

Authority Must Be Clear

It wasn't a big moment.
That's what made it easy to miss.

Two adults.
Same space.
Same situation.

A simple question.

"Can I do this?"

Answered once.
"Yes."

Answered again.
"No."

Same question.
Different answer.

And right there,
everything shifted.

Not loudly.
But completely.

Because now,
it wasn't about the question.

It was about the system.

And the system just broke.
That's what inconsistency between adults does.
It doesn't just create confusion.
It removes authority.

Because authority isn't just what's said.
It's what's aligned.

And alignment,
is what makes something real.

Without it,
everything becomes negotiable.

When two authorities exist,
people don't choose the stricter one.
They choose the inconsistent one.

Because inconsistency creates opportunity.
And opportunity gets explored.

That's human.
That's system response.

Because when authority isn't clear,
people don't follow it.
They navigate it.
They search for it.
They test it.

Not to be difficult.
To find the version that works for them.

And once that happens,
you're no longer leading.

You're recovering.

Because leadership happens before the moment.
Correction happens after it.

And most households are living in correction.
Because nothing was aligned before.

That's the gap.

Because authority doesn't fail just from inconsistency.
It fails from lack of ownership.

When no one clearly owns the system,
authority gets borrowed.
One person sets the tone.
Another adjusts to it.

And instead of alignment,
you get interpretation.

That's where things break.

Because borrowed clarity doesn't create authority.
It creates variation.

And variation creates instability.

Authority cannot exist inside a system no one owns.

Because authority is not about control.
It's about consistency.

And consistency only comes from:
clarity
ownership
structure

That's what makes it real.

That's what makes it hold.

This isn't about being more authoritative.

It's about removing anything that makes authority unclear.

Because unclear authority,
will always be challenged.

What's aligned,
becomes predictable.

And what's predictable,
becomes respected.

Not because it's demanded.
Because it's experienced.

Clear.
Aligned.
Unmoving.

If it depends on who you ask,
it's not authority.
It's preference.

And preference,
gets negotiated.

This isn't about stronger authority.

It's about clearer authority.

And clarity,
is what makes it hold.

CHAPTER 17

Systems Hold What People Can't

Coats by the door.
Bags half-packed.
Someone still looking for a shoe.

We were supposed to leave ten minutes ago.

And I was holding all of it.
The timeline.
The checklist.
The sequence of what needed to happen and in what order.

All of it.
In my head.
Nowhere else.

A simple expectation.
Something that had already been said.

And then,
it didn't happen.

Not dramatically.
Just... missed.

And I felt it.

That familiar pull.

Do I address it?
Do I let it go?

And right there,
was the real problem.

Not the behavior.
The decision.

Because if every moment requires a decision,
nothing is actually decided.

That's the system.
Or more accurately,
the absence of one.

Because when something depends on you,
it's not stable.

It's conditional.
Conditional on your energy.
Your attention.
Your timing.

And anything conditional,
will eventually break.

That's what I had been doing.
Holding everything.
In real time.

Every expectation.
Every boundary.
Every correction.

Carried.
Moment by moment.

And it worked,
until it didn't.

Because people can't hold what systems should.

That's the shift.

This isn't about being more consistent.

It's about building something that is.

Because consistency is not a personality trait.
It's a system outcome.

That's where most people get stuck.

They try to become more disciplined.
More present.
More on top of things.

But that's not scalable.

Because people fluctuate.
Systems don't.

That's the difference.

When a system is in place,
it holds.
Without you reminding it.
Without you re-explaining it.

It just stays.

That's what creates stability.
Not effort.

Structure.

Because effort runs out.
Structure doesn't.

That's when everything clicked.

I didn't need to show up better.
I needed to build something that didn't depend on how I showed up.

Because systems do three things people can't:
They make things visible.
They make things consistent.
They make things predictable.

And predictability changes behavior.

Because when something is predictable,
people adjust to it.
Not question it.

That's what removes friction.
Not control.
Clarity.

And clarity,
is what systems create.

That's when I stopped asking:
"How do I handle this better?"

And started asking:
"What system would make this unnecessary?"

That question changes everything.

Because it removes you from the center.
And puts structure in its place.

That's where things stabilize.

Because now,
the system holds it.
Not you.

The framework is simple.
Alignment creates clarity.
Clarity defines authority.
Authority stabilizes behavior.
And systems,
hold all of it.

Miss one,
everything weakens.

Have all four,
everything stabilizes.

That's not theory.
That's design.

And design,
is what makes outcomes predictable.

This isn't behavior.

It's about what holds behavior in place.

And behavior only holds,
when something stronger than the moment exists.

That something,
is a system.

And systems hold what people can't.

. . .

CHAPTER 18

What You're Actually Building

It was something small.
The kind I used to move past.

A recurring charge.
Roblox.
$9.99.

And I remember thinking,
I could just cancel it.

That used to be the move.
Fix the charge.
Maybe say something.
Let it go.

But this time I paused.

Because it wasn't about the $9.99.

It was a visibility problem.
A duplication problem across households.
An authority gap.

And what hit me wasn't the charge,
it was how quickly I could see the system underneath it.

No frustration.

No second-guessing if it was my place.
Just:
this is a structure issue.
And here's how we fix it.

I remember realizing,
I used to overthink moments like this.

I don't anymore.

That's the part most people don't notice about the work.

You don't announce when the shift happens.
You just... move differently.

Handle things with less weight.
See patterns instead of problems.
Ask different questions.

And one day you realize,
you've been building something.

Not overnight.
Not perfectly.
But consistently.

Because nothing is isolated.
Not in a system.

Every moment connects.
Every decision carries forward.
Every response reinforces something.

Whether you see it,
or not.

That's the part most people miss.

They think they're managing moments.
They're not.

They're building patterns.

And patterns,
become systems.

And systems,
produce outcomes.

That's the chain.
Not complicated.
But constant.

Because systems don't wait for intention.
They form from repetition.

And repetition,
creates structure.

Whether you designed it,
or not.

Once I saw that,
everything felt heavier.
Not in a negative way.
In a real way.

Because now,
every small moment mattered.

Not because of what it was.
Because of what it was building.

That's the part that changes you.

When you realize,

you're not just raising kids.
You're shaping how they understand the world.

Through what you reinforce.
Through what you allow.
Through what you make clear,
and what you leave undefined.

That's what they take with them.

Not what you say.
What you consistently do.

That's what forms identity.
Not in one moment.
Across many.

That's why this matters.

Not because of today.
Because of what today becomes.

Over time.
Repeated.
Reinforced.
Normalized.

That's how standards are built.
Quietly.
Without announcement.
Without intention.

Until one day,
it's just how things are.

This isn't about getting through the day.

It's about what the day is producing.

Because production is always happening.
Even when you're not paying attention.

This isn't management.

It's construction.

And construction,
requires design.

Because what you don't design,
will default.

And default systems rarely produce what you actually want.

That's why this matters.

Not for control.
For direction.

Because direction determines outcome.

And outcome,
doesn't happen later.

It's being built now.
In small moments.
Repeated.

. . .

CHAPTER 19

The Adults They Become

It wasn't happening in the moment.
That's what made it easy to miss.

Nothing looked wrong.
No major issue.
No obvious failure.

Just normal behavior.
Normal responses.
Normal patterns.

And that's what stopped me.

Because normal,
is what becomes permanent.

That's the part most people don't question.
They look for problems.
Big ones.
Obvious ones.

And if they don't see them,
they assume everything is fine.

But the truth is,
what looks normal today...
becomes identity tomorrow.

That's how it works.
Not through big moments.
Through repeated ones.

What's allowed.
What's expected.
What's reinforced.

Over time,
it forms something.

Not behavior.
Belief.

And belief,
is what drives everything else.

How they think.
How they decide.
What they tolerate.

That's what carries forward.
Not the rule.
The pattern behind it.

That's the shift.

You're not just influencing behavior.
You're shaping belief.

And belief,
doesn't stay in your house.

It moves.

Into relationships.
Into work.

Into every system they enter.

That's what you're actually building.
Not compliance.
Capacity.

Because the goal isn't to control behavior now.
It's to prepare them for environments where you're not there.

That's where it shows.
When no one is watching.
When no one is correcting.

What do they default to?

That's the system you built.
Not what you said.
What you reinforced.

Shape: A moment where you saw the system living in one of the kids without prompting. Suggested: A child who navigated something , a decision, a situation , the way the structure taught them. You recognized it. You felt it. That's the image.]

And then there was the morning he asked permission
to get a cookie from the kitchen.

Not because he feared punishment.
Not because he was checking the rules.

But because that's simply how he understands the world now.

Access has process.
Even for cookies.

My heart fluttered with his innocence.

Because that flutter wasn't just warmth.
It was recognition.

That's the system.
That's what I built.
And it's inside him now,
without me having to hold it there.

That's the truth about this work.

It doesn't announce itself.
It just lives in them.

In the questions they ask.
In the way they pause before acting.
In the moment they think before they take.

That's what compounds.
Into habits.
Into standards.
Into identity.

That's how adults are formed.
Not in big decisions.
In small ones.
Repeated.

This isn't about behavior.

It's about belief.

And belief,
is what becomes who they are.

. . .

CHAPTER 20

The Standard You Set

It wasn't said out loud.
No announcement.
No agreement.

And still,
it existed.

The standard.

You could feel it.

In what was allowed.
In what was corrected.
In what was ignored.

That's how standards form.
Not through words.
Through patterns.

Because people don't follow what's said once.
They follow what stays consistent.

That's the standard.
Not what you intend.
What you repeat.

That's the shift.

Because most people think they're setting standards,
when they're actually setting exceptions.

Just this once.
Not right now.
It's not a big deal.

And individually,
those moments feel small.

But collectively,
they build something.

Flexibility without clarity.

And that creates confusion.

Because now,
nothing feels fixed.
Everything feels adjustable.

And when everything feels adjustable,
nothing feels real.

That's the problem.
Not behavior.
Stability.

Because standards don't form from what you say.
They form from what doesn't change.

That's what people trust.
That's what people organize around.
That's what people internalize.

And once a standard is formed,
it's hard to undo.

Because now it's not a rule.
It's a baseline.

That's what people expect.
That's what they operate from.

And changing a baseline,
is harder than setting one.

That's why this matters.
Not in big moments.
In small ones.

Repeated.

Because repetition,
is what defines the standard.

Not intention.
Not explanation.

Repetition.

This isn't about what you say.

It's about what you make consistent.

Because what you make consistent,
becomes the standard.

And the standard,
is what shapes everything else.

. . .

CHAPTER 21

The System You Leave Behind

We were at dinner.

Different night.
Same table.

The phone question came up again.
It always does.

But this time,
I watched instead of reacted.

And I noticed something I hadn't seen before.

Before I could say anything,
one of the kids looked at another.

A glance.
Just that.

And the phone went away.

Not because I said something.
Not because there was a consequence coming.

Because they knew.

Because the standard had been set enough times
that it no longer needed to be held.

It just existed.

That's the moment.
The one that matters most.

Not because it was dramatic.
Because it wasn't.

Because when you're not there,
when you're not in the room,
when you're not available to remind or correct or redirect,

only two things remain.

The structure.
Or the absence of it.

And that night,
the structure was there.

Without me holding it.

That's the legacy.

Not what you taught.
What held.

Because what holds,
continues.

Without you.
Beyond the moment.
Beyond the house.

Into every environment they walk into.
Every system they're part of.
Every decision they make when no one is watching.

That's what you're building toward.

Not to be needed in every moment.
But to build something that doesn't need you.

That's leadership.
Not control.
Continuity.

Because if everything depends on you,
it disappears when you do.

But if it's built into the system,
it stays.

That's where everything connects.

Alignment.
Authority.
Behavior.
Systems.

All of it,
working together.
Not in one moment.
Across all of them.

That's what creates stability.
That's what creates identity.
That's what creates legacy.

Not by accident.
By design.

This isn't about raising kids.

It's about building a system,
that raises them when you're not there.

That's the work.
That's the responsibility.
That's the opportunity.

Because what you leave behind,
won't be your words.

It will be your system.
And your system,
is what they will carry forward.

Into every decision.
Every environment.
Every version of who they become.

This isn't parenting.

This is legacy design.

. . .

CLOSING

There won't be a moment when everything suddenly feels finished.

No clear line.
No final test.
No point where you think,
I got it perfect.

That's not how this works.

Because this was never about perfection.
It was about awareness.

And once you have it,
you can't give it back.

You won't unsee inconsistency.
You won't ignore ambiguity.
You won't mistake behavior,
for what's actually producing it.

That's the shift.
Not in what you do.
In how you see.

Because once you see the system,
you stop reacting to moments.

You start designing them.

And that changes everything.

Think about the last moment that derailed you.
The tone that shifted the room.
The question that turned into a negotiation.
The evening that started clean and ended tense.

Now think about what was missing underneath it.

Not the behavior.
The structure.

Because you know now what you didn't know before.
That tension lives in the gaps.
In the ambiguity.
In the spaces where nothing has been decided.

And you know how to close those gaps.

Not with more effort.
With design.

You know what visibility does.
You know what consistency builds.
You know what happens when authority is clear,
and what happens when it isn't.

You know the difference between control and structure.
Between keeping the peace and reinforcing instability.
Between borrowed clarity and owned clarity.

And that knowledge,
doesn't stay theoretical.

It starts showing up in small moments.
The pause before you respond.
The question you ask instead of the answer you give.
The boundary you hold without over-explaining.

The standard you keep,
because you know what it's building.

And over time,
what once felt hard...
becomes stable.

Not because life got easier.
Because the system got stronger.

That's what you've built.

Not just better moments.
Better structure.

Not just clearer expectations.
Clearer systems.

And systems,
are what make everything else work.

That's what holds when you're tired.
When you're busy.
When you don't have the energy to explain it again.

Because now,
it doesn't depend on you.

That's the goal.
Not to carry everything.
To build something that carries itself.

That's leadership.
Not loud.
Not forceful.
Designed.

Because what's designed,
lasts.

Not perfect.
Predictable.

Not rigid.
Stable.

Not controlled.
Clear.

And clarity,
is what allows everything else to grow.

This isn't parenting.

This is architecture.

And now,
you know how to build.